Alexander Climbs a Maple Tree

by Vicky Ann Meier

Published 2025

Printed in the United States of America

First Edition
ISBN (softcover): 978-1-963380-30-9
ISBN (hardcover): 978-1-963380-79-8
ISBN (e-book): 978-1-963380-80-4

For information, address:
Holzer Books LLC
8 The Green, Ste. A
Dover, Delaware 19901 USA

For information about special discounts available for bulk purchases, sales promotions, and educational needs, contact: info@holzerbooksllc.com or +1 (888) 901-7776

This book is dedicated to my three children whose love and support made this journey possible.

Alexander is a gray cat with big ears and a patch of white around one eye.

Others used to make fun of his ears, but his best friend Ellie thinks they suit him and that he is the perfect cat for her.

Ellie and Alexander love to go outside to play.
There is so much to see, so many places to explore!

Sometimes Alexander would stray away a bit while chasing a bird or a butterfly, and Ellie would call him to come back.

One time he didn't come back right away,
and it started to rain.

He came home very wet,
which he didn't like at all, then had to
stay inside the house for many days.

He didn't like being inside while Ellie was outside, so now he always comes when Ellie calls.

One day they went outside because Ellie wanted to
pick some flowers for her room.

She and her mother had planted wildflowers
in the back yard just for Ellie.

Alexander liked exploring in the wildflowers
because the bumblebees and butterflies liked them too,
and it was fun to watch them and chase them.

He never did catch one,
but he enjoyed trying.

That day a butterfly that Alexander was chasing flew around the house to the front yard.

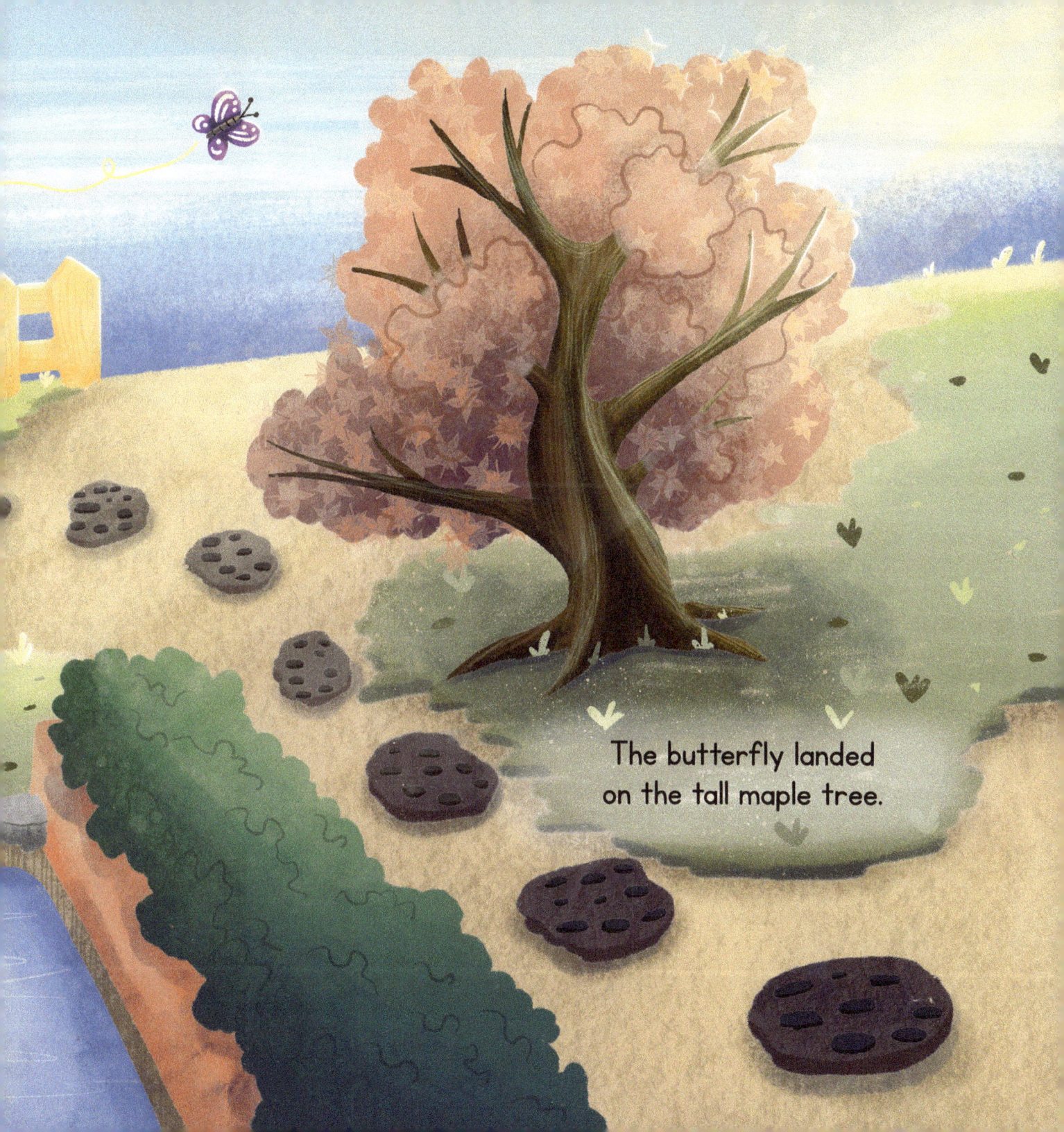

The butterfly landed
on the tall maple tree.

Without thinking, Alexander climbed up
the maple tree to the branch where he
saw the butterfly.

But just as he reached the branch,
the butterfly flew to a higher branch.
Alexander climbed higher to that branch.
Again, the butterfly flew to an
even higher branch.

Alexander followed the butterfly higher...

and higher...

and higher...

until the butterfly landed at
the top of the tall maple tree.

Just as Alexander reached the top of the tree the butterfly flew off to find more wildflowers.

Alexander peeked out from the tree and could see over the roof to the backyard where Ellie was picking wildflowers. He decided he should go back to Ellie because she would wonder where he had gone to.

He looked down and
"yikes!!"

Alexander was great at climbing up,
but he didn't know how to climb down.
He was afraid he would fall.

He looked out again at Ellie.

"Meow!", he cried.

"Meow!"

Ellie looked around.
"Alexander, is that you I hear?
Where are you?"

He kept crying

"Meow"

and Ellie followed his voice
to the front yard.

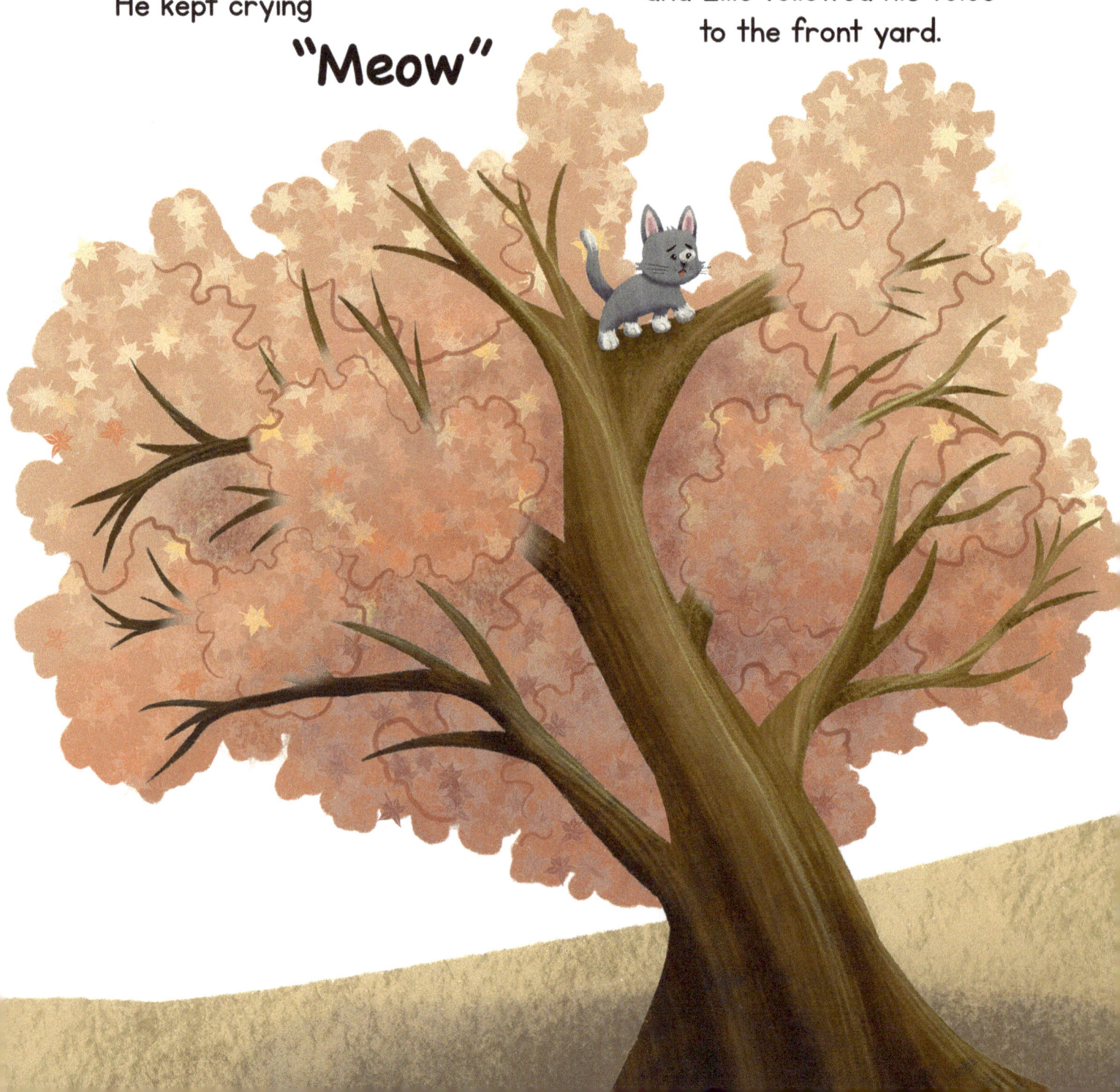

He answered with a loud

"Meow!"

She came to the maple tree and said,
"Alexander, where are you?"

Ellie looked up into the tall maple tree.
"Alexander, there you are! Poor kitty!
I will help you down."

Now Ellie was a very
brave girl and was very
good at climbing trees.

The tall maple tree was her
favorite climbing tree.
Alexander knew she could
help him down.

He watched as she climbed higher...

and higher...

and higher, until she finally reached
the top of the maple tree.

She took Alexander and hugged him close to her.
Alexander was so happy to see her
but still afraid to be so high in the tree.

Ellie tucked Alexander safely inside her
shirt so he wouldn't have to look down,
then started climbing down.

When they reached the ground
Ellie hugged Alexander and said,
"Oh Alexander, you silly kitty.
No more climbing the maple tree, okay?"

Alexander snuggled against his girl and purred.
He agreed, no more climbing the maple tree.
From now on he would stay on the ground to
chase the butterflies.

to be continued...

About the Author

After working nearly 25 years in the senior living field, Vicky retired and currently lives in her home state of Indiana. She enjoys time with family, walking, and road trips with her beloved dog Mikey. Her children's books share themes of friendship, responsibility, and spreading everyday kindness.

About the illustrator

Mentari enjoys creating illustrations with whimsical, vintage pencil effects that bring beautiful childhood memories.

www.ingramcontent.com/pod-product-compliance
Lightning Source LLC
Chambersburg PA
CBHW041601260326
41914CB00011B/1338

9 781963 380798